PAST AND PRESENT

HOMELESSNESS

CAROLE SEYMOUR-JONES

new Discovery B·O·O·K·S

New York

First American publication 1993 by New Discovery Books, Macmillan Publishing Company, 866 Third Avenue, New York, NY 10022

Macmillan Publishing Company is part of the Maxwell Communication Group of Companies

First published in 1993 by Heinemann Library, an imprint of Heinemann Educational, a division of Heinemann Publishers (Oxford) Ltd, Halley Court, Jordan Hill, Oxford OX2 8EJ

Devised and produced by Zoë Books Limited
15 Worthy Lane, Winchester, SO23 7AB, England

Edited by Charlotte Rolfe
Picture research by Faith Perkins
Designed by Julian Holland

Printed in China

Library of Congress Cataloging-in-Publication Data
Seymour-Jones, Carole.
    Homelessness / Carole Seymour-Jones.
        p. cm. — (Past and present)
    Includes index.
    Summary: Examines the phenomenon of homelessness from its first
recorded appearance in 448 b.c. to the present word-wide crisis.
    ISBN 0-02-786882-6
    1. Homelessness — History — Juvenile literature. 2. Homeless persons —
History — Juvenile literature. [1. Homelessness.] I. Title. II. Series.
    HV4480.549 1993
    362.5'09 — dc20
                                                        92-39445

Photographic acknowledgments

The author and publishers wish to acknowledge, with thanks, the following photographic sources: Hulton-Deutsch Collection pp 13; 17; 21; 22; 26: IMPACT pp title page; 29; 37: Magnum pp 15 (Bischof); 19 (Mayer); 34 (Nichols); 36 (Mayer); 39 (Mendel): Musee des Beaux-Arts, Lausanne p 11: Peter Newark's Western Americana pp 9; 31: Rex Features pp 4; 7; 24; 43.

The cover photograph is courtesy of Magnum/Chris Steele Perkins.

Title page: **The sign around this man's neck explains that he is homeless and therefore has to ask for help from passersby. He is one of the many homeless people on the streets of New York City today.**

CONTENTS

WITHOUT A HOME

A disabled woman boils water for a warm drink on a Moscow pavement during the spring of 1990. Huge political and economic changes in Russia have wiped out many people's jobs and savings. Hospitals and residential homes have been closed, and former patients have been forced out onto the streets.

It is April in Bombay and the temperature is over 110°F. Huddled figures lie asleep on the pavements as the traffic swirls around them. Small children run back and forth, while old women squat on wooden beds grinding spices. Cooking, eating, washing, and sleeping are all done on the street, for in Bombay, one of the largest cities in India, many thousands of people have no other homes.

Twenty years ago two brothers came to Bombay because there was a drought in their home region of Sholapur. This forced their father to sell his two acres of land to a bigger farmer. The boys, aged 17 and 13, hopped on the train without paying and came to the big city to find work. They slept in the open air on the pavement. Now, years later, they are both married. "There is no going back to the village," they say. "We would go back, but not our children."

Newspapers and television bring the issue of homelessness into comfortable homes in the West. They show the contrast between the "haves" and "have-nots" of the **First** and **Third World** countries. But homelessness is not found only in poor countries: it can be found in the heart of the world's richer countries, such as the United States and Great Britain.

In Britain more than 125,000 families were officially recorded as homeless in 1989 — over 15 percent more than in the previous year. Thousands of parents and children live in temporary accommodations, cramped bed and breakfast hotels, run-down hostels, and decaying trailers. Young single people who are not described as officially homeless live on the streets of London in cardboard boxes and tents. Many more "hidden homeless" live as **squatters** in abandoned houses or move around, sleeping on the floors of friends' homes.

WHAT'S IN A WORD?
Dictionaries define a homeless person as "having no home or permanent abode." In Old English the world "home" meant a village with its cottages. Yet today in many cultures home does not mean the bricks and mortar of a high-rise city apartment or a row of neat houses and

gardens along a tree-lined avenue. For the Masai in Kenya a home is a hut made of mud and dung, for the Marsh Arabs of southern Iraq a dwelling is created of reeds from the Tigris River.

"Home" need not be a fixed spot either. **Nomadic** peoples like the Tuareg and Bella in the Sahara Desert live in leather tents and often move camp in search of water and pasture for their cattle and goats, piling all their belongings on to the backs of donkeys or camels.

The first human beings on earth were hunters and gatherers who followed their prey for food and had no fixed dwellings; they lived in caves or temporary shelters. From about 7000 B.C., people discovered how to grow corn and raise animals. They began building settlements around rivers, where there was a good supply of water for drinking and watering crops and herds. The first civilizations developed. More than 4,000 years ago the peoples of the Indus valley in India were living in houses made of bricks. These houses were grouped together in settlements with a pattern of streets and covered drains.

Many types of dwellings have served as homes at different times in the past, and in different parts of the world, but to be accepted as "home" by their inhabitants, they generally meet certain needs. A home is not just a building. It is also made up by the people who live in it and by their relationship to one another and to the place where they live. So the idea of a home is an emotional one. However, without the basic shelter and security of a reasonable dwelling place, it is very difficult to build up that idea of home.

"Mid pleasures and palaces tho' we roam,
Be it ever so humble, there's no place like home . . .
Home, home, sweet, sweet home!
There's no place like home! There's no place like home!"

From Clari, the Maid of Milan
by J.H. Payne (1791–1852)

For the Masai, home and security depend on their cattle. The people move over great distances with their animals in search of new grazing. To the Masai, this may mean "moving house" as well.

A home also has to provide an economic base for its occupants. People need to be able to make a living in the place where they settle. Once this is no longer possible, the home often breaks up.

The occupants of a dwelling may be a large, **extended family**, a **nuclear family** of parents and children, single parents and children, or people living alone. Ideally a dwelling should be within reach of work, clean water, transportation, and traders or stores so that people can form a community and children can go to school. A dwelling should offer protection, too. In northern climates it is important to protect people from the cold, while in the south, houses are built to offer protection from the sun. In this way the **environment** may influence the type of dwelling that people choose.

Different ideas about home have developed through the

centuries, often inspired by religious ideas. In the **Middle Ages** monasteries and convents offered shelter to many thousands of monks and nuns, and in the twentieth century religious communes also attract people who want to live in a particular group according to certain rules or principles.

It has been a tradition of all the major religions to offer shelter and safety to the homeless, but in the nineteenth and twentieth centuries national governments have often taken over this role. Orphans and people with mental illnesses are often **segregated** from the rest of society in institutions that may be called "homes." A hostel may provide a halfway house for teenagers who leave the family home in their search for independence.

The right to a home is a basic human right, essential for human dignity. Yet today there are more people than ever before in history who are homeless, and the gap between the homeless and the housed is widening. Still, in most countries, housing is at the bottom of the political agenda.

WAR VICTIMS

During the Civil War (1861–1865), many thousands of civilians were caught up in the crossfire. They lost their homes, and often their lives. This picture shows the destruction of the railroad and the burning of the city of Atlanta by Federal troops in 1864.

War has been one of the main causes of homelessness for thousands of years. People have fled in terror as armies advance and plunder their food supplies or set fire to their villages. Nevertheless, before the invention of guns in the fourteenth century, war was on a smaller scale. The twentieth century, on the other hand, is often called the century of "total war."

PLUNDER AND SIEGE IN ANCIENT GREECE

The city-state of Athens relied on its powerful navy to keep control of the many islands in the eastern Mediterranean. Any opposition was ruthlessly put down. In the middle of the fifth century B.C., the Athenians took over the Greek island of Evvoia, drove out the local people, and gave their lands and homes to poorer Athenians who they felt could be relied upon to stay loyal to Athens.

Not long afterward, though, Athens found itself at war with the neighboring state of Sparta. The war lasted for ten years, from 431 B.C.. During the first year of fighting, many people had to flee their homes in the countryside and take shelter within the city of Athens itself. Many fell ill and died from a **plague** that spread more violently because the city was so overcrowded.

ROMANS IN BRITAIN

The Roman Empire was far larger and more powerful than the Greek civilization that it followed. It stretched right across Europe. Roman soldiers guarded its boundaries from North Africa to Britain.

The Roman occupation of Britain was recorded in some detail by the Roman historian, Tacitus. He described how the Romans drove the native Celtic people from their homes and land and called them prisoners and slaves. The Celts were forced to build a temple to the Roman emperor, Claudius, at Camulodunum (now Colchester, England) in about A.D. 60.

A local queen, Boudicca, led her people against the Romans, and sacked the city of Colchester. The mud and timber houses were burned and the inhabitants massacred. Boudicca led her army on to Londinium, the

Roman capital in Britain, and burned the city to the ground. More than 70,000 Romans were killed. Those who remained alive fled with whatever possessions they could rescue from the terrible fire that raged throughout the city.

ON THE RAMPAGE

War machines were developed and strengthened throughout the Middle Ages. Firearms in the field made armies more and more difficult to conquer. During the bloodthirsty Thirty Years' War between Protestants and Catholics (1618–1648), Germany was torn apart by **civil war**, and country people were helpless at the hands of competing armies living "off the land." Soldiers would turn peasants out of their homes at gunpoint or burn their farms if they did not feed and house the fighting men. In

This massacre of French Protestants took place in Paris on Saint Bartholomew's Day (August 23) in 1572. It added to the hatred between Protestants and Catholics in 16th-century France, and set off a chain of attacks in which many Protestants had to flee their homes.

1631 the city of Magdeburg was surrounded by troops. Desperate to find provisions for his starving soldiers, the Catholic general, Tilly, besieged Magdeburg because its granaries were bulging with grain. Cannons battered the city walls and the houses within, and when, after four weeks, the city fell, the people and their homes were burned. Only 5,000 out of the 30,000 inhabitants survived, and the city was left a ruin. Unfortunately for Tilly, even the granaries had been destroyed.

BURNING OUT THE OPPOSITION

Burning people's homes has remained a popular way of punishing the enemy in the twentieth century. One of the most ruthless armed bands earlier this century were the British "Black and Tans," a special division of the police force in Ireland. In 1920 centuries of English rule in Ireland were beginning to come to an end in a fierce guerrilla war between the "Black and Tans" and the Irish Republican Army (IRA).

The Black and Tans (their name described the color of their uniforms) were mostly recruited from English soldiers. They were much less disciplined than the main police force in Ireland, and often carried out terrible punishments on local people as reprisals against IRA attacks on their strongholds. In one small town alone, 25 houses were burned down and their occupants driven out by the Black and Tans. Creameries, or dairies, were burned down, too, as a means of putting people out of work. In December 1920 the Black and Tans burned the center of the city of Cork as a punishment for an ambush by the IRA.

In 1922 Ireland finally broke free from British rule, and an independent republic was declared. But in the separate province of Ulster, or Northern Ireland, which is still part of the United Kingdom, similar terror tactics continue to be used by extreme political groups.

TERROR FROM THE SKY

During the years of World War II (1939–1945) millions of people lost their homes. At various stages during the war,

The morning after a German bomb raid during August 1940.
This London family survived the attack, but they had to leave
their home with what few possessions they could rescue from
the ruins.

Nazi Germany carried out bombing campaigns on a number of British cities. Two out of every seven houses were destroyed in these attacks, the worst of which happened in 1940, and was known as "the Blitz" (from the German word for lightning).

Londoners were bombed for 76 nights in a row during the Blitz. Sleeping in shelters or in underground railroad stations became a way of life for many people. Others, especially children, were **evacuated**, or sent to safety, in the country. For some, this was an unhappy experience. However, it was also a lesson for the future, since it made many people more aware of the poverty that existed in parts of the big cities. This was to lead to big improvements in housing, health, and education in later years.

In the meantime, as the war entered its final stages, even more drastic bombing raids were carried out by the Allied (British and American) forces on German cities. The bombing of Dresden caused a terrible fire that was so powerful it pulled people back into it as they tried to escape. Later on many people questioned the purpose and justification for these raids on helpless civilians.

By the end of the war, over 7 million Germans were homeless. Many had been bombed out, and others had fled from the Soviet army's advance toward Berlin. Over the previous five years, many small towns and villages in eastern Europe and western Russia had been totally destroyed by advancing and retreating armies belonging to either Germany or the Soviet Union. For the survivors there was little chance of ever returning home.

THE FINAL HORROR

In order to force Japan to surrender at the end of the war, the Allies decided to drop the world's first atomic bomb on Hiroshima, an important seaport and military base on the southern Japanese island of Honshu.

The bomb was dropped from an American B29 in the early morning of August 6, 1945. When it exploded, an immense fireball was created, reaching a diameter of more than 650 feet in less than a second. Many thousands of

This picture shows the level of damage caused by the atomic bomb dropped on the Japanese city of Hiroshima at the end of World War II.

people perished instantly, and those who survived were left with terrible injuries caused by the effects of **radiation**. Over three-fifths of the city was destroyed by this single attack, and there was hardly a building that remained undamaged. Although the city was rebuilt after the war and is now a modern industrial center, it contains a memorial to those who suffered.

''The heaven burnt red, and my body also melted away! Please cry with Hiroshima.''

Epitaph for atom bomb victims, Hiroshima memorial

WAITING TO RETURN

Wars still make people homeless in many parts of the world today. The 1991 Gulf War displaced thousands of people in Iraq and Kuwait. Many non-Kuwaitis who were living and working in Kuwait at the start of the war were too frightened to return to their homes afterward. Among these were several thousand Palestinians. They felt it was safer to stay in overcrowded, makeshift conditions with relations in friendly neighboring countries such as Jordan than to return to places where they might be viewed with suspicion as outsiders or even be accused of siding with the enemy. War rarely increases the safety or security of groups such as these, even though it is known that many Palestinians bravely resisted the invasion for as long as they were able.

In the northeast African country of Somalia, more than 250,000 people were left homeless by the terrible civil war that broke out in 1991. One of these refugees, Hawa Deria, describes her experience when the war hit Mogadishu, the Somali capital, that November.

"There was bombing and shooting all around. I said to my mother, 'We have to leave.' She said, 'Let's wait,' so we waited one more day. Then a bomb hit the house next door, killing all their children. We had to go — all of us."

Hawa Deria and her family managed to escape to Ethiopia, where they ended up in a refugee camp. But for this family, and many others, it may be months or even years before it is possible to return home. Even then, it can mean rebuilding a house, struggling to work on land that has become overgrown, renewing clean water supplies, and re-creating a community. The task is enormous, but for many who are waiting to return, the will is even greater.

ACCIDENTS AND DISASTERS

The city of San Francisco in California was struck by a massive earthquake in 1906. About 250,000 people were made homeless.

Even now, in the late twentieth century, we are often powerless when natural disasters occur. Our knowledge of science and technology cannot fully protect us from earthquakes, storms, and fire. Other disasters are caused by human error. Sometimes these accidents also cause widespread death and suffering, including homelessness.

A VOLCANO ERUPTS

In the first century A.D., the people of Pompeii, a seaside city near Naples in southern Italy, lived in the shadow of a volcano — Mount Vesuvius. They were used to the volcano, which they believed to be extinct, and had forgotten that it meant danger.

On a summer's day in A.D. 79, a strong rumbling sound was heard. This was followed by a steady rain of white ash that fell from a cloud at the top of the mountain. Finally, after about 24 hours, the volcano erupted. About 2,000 people who had sheltered in their homes were suffocated by the volcano's poisonous gases. Those who had escaped by sea or by fleeing inland returned to find their houses buried several feet deep under the ash. Pompeii had simply ceased to exist, along with the homes of its 20,000 inhabitants. Many of those who returned tried to dig up their possessions from the ashes after the ground had cooled, but most of the city remained preserved and forgotten for hundreds of years until it was excavated in the eighteenth century.

THE LONG JOURNEY

The island of Tristan da Cunha is probably one of the loneliest places on earth. It sits in the middle of the South Atlantic Ocean, with a tiny British population descended from the soldiers who guarded Napoleon on St. Helena, many miles to the north. The island is only six miles across, rising in the center to a volcanic peak.

In 1961 the volcano erupted, and the 264 islanders had to be taken off by fishing boats; they abandoned their thatched stone houses for new homes thousands of miles away in England. In 1962 the volcano was quiet again. The islanders voted to go home. England was strange to them, and although they had been rehoused, it was not the buildings but the familiar life of keeping cattle and sheep, growing potatoes, and fishing, for which they were homesick. They disliked England's big cities and its cold climate. During 1963 and 1964 nearly all the islanders returned.

EARTHQUAKES

Active volcanoes are located on the two earthquake belts, one encircling the Pacific Ocean and the other reaching across southern Asia through the Mediterranean Sea to Africa. In California many people live on the San Andreas fault — an unsettled part of the earth's crust — that caused the 1906 San Francisco earthquake. It is human nature to be optimistic, so people continue to live in areas where there is a possible threat to their homes and lives. Many of the world's big cities such as Tokyo, Istanbul, and Mexico City are situated in earthquake risk areas.

In 1988 the Armenian city of Leninakan was flattened by an earthquake that killed many thousands of people and left nearly two million homeless in mid-winter conditions. Here, rescue workers are wearing masks and plastic suits to protect them from the dust and smells. After ten days, there were few survivors, but many mourners.

NO ONE AT HOME

Sometimes homelessness can be caused by widespread sickness. An epidemic may rob a community of its entire work force. What happens then?

In the middle of the fourteenth century most of Europe and the countries around the Mediterranean were struck by a terrible plague known as the Black Death. In England alone it killed over one in four people. Whole villages were abandoned because there was no one to cultivate the land. Fields were soon covered with weeds and cottages fell into ruins; today aerial photographs show where these villages used to stand.

FAMINE

In the nineteenth century, ruined villages in Ireland were evidence of a different sort. For many centuries Ireland suffered under the control of rich landowners who neglected their farm tenants, many of whom lived in extremely poor conditions. Matters were made worse when in 1845 much of the potato crop was destroyed by a disease. The following year, there was no crop at all. The poor had nothing left to eat and no money to pay rent.

Although some landowners did their best to help the families in the cottages on their estates, many saw the famine as an excuse to get rid of the responsibility of unwanted tenants. Thousands of poor country dwellers found themselves on the road. They were faced with a cold winter and a lack of suitable clothing and shelter. Many fell sick with fever and died. Many more struggled to escape by ship to England, Canada, or the United States. Those who might have helped them often turned away because they were frightened of catching the fever.

> "Hundreds of poor people . . . huddled together without light, without air, sick in body, dispirited in heart . . . fevered patients lying beside the sound, by their agonised ravings disturbing those around."
>
> *Stephen de Vere, passenger on board a "coffin ship" bound for North America, 1847*

Soup is distributed to the poor and homeless in the town of Cork during the Irish famine of 1847. Although many groups and individuals worked hard to provide support, relief came too late for most people in Ireland.

FIRE!

Fire is perhaps one of the most common disasters that can make people homeless. In 1666 a fire that started in a baker's shop raced through the city of London within hours. The wooden houses in the narrow, overcrowded streets burned easily, and the terrible fire lasted for four days. People took to the Thames River in boats with whatever belongings they could gather. Only when the fire was over could the damage be counted. Over 13,000 homes had been destroyed — most of old London in fact.

> "Here we saw carts carrying goods out to the fields . . . and tents erected to shelter both people and what goods they could get away."
>
> *Entry for September 3, 1666,*
> *from the diary of John Evelyn (1620–1706)*

This drawing of old London shows most of the city on the northern bank of the Thames River ablaze in the great fire of 1666.

Although many people lost their homes, the fire did give Londoners a chance to rebuild the old part of the city. Wide new streets were planned, and fine buildings such as St. Paul's Cathedral were designed and built.

WALLS OF WATER

These big disasters do not always result in improvements for the future. In many parts of the world homes are repeatedly destroyed by rivers in full flood or by tidal waves that are caused by earthquakes taking place under the sea.

In the southern part of Bangladesh, many thousands of people live on the flat land around the mouth of the Ganges River. Floods are a constant hazard, but the people continue to live and farm the land there, because the demand for farmland is very great and there is nowhere else to go. In 1991 a tidal wave destroyed nearly 800,000 homes in the area, but the survivors still came back.

Today the people living around the lower Ganges suffer

from regular floods that come from upriver. In the hills to the north, huge areas of forest have been cleared for lumber. The trees that would normally have held the rainfall in the land are no longer there. So millions of tons of rainwater rush straight into the rivers during the rainy season. As the muddy water flows down to the sea it no longer waters the crops on the southern plains — it washes them away, together with homes and villages.

The floods in Bangladesh show how accidents and disasters very often have their roots in changes people make to their environment. By the time the connection between the cause and effect is recognized, it can be too late.

LOOKING FOR WORK

This ruined cottage is all that remains of a former home on the coast of Donegal in the west of Ireland. Over several centuries, people have turned their backs on extreme poverty and risked homelessness in faraway cities and new countries.

From about 1760 a process of economic change known as the **industrial revolution** took place in England. Over the next 80 years the machine age came into being. The land changed as people left their villages to live in new factory towns. New technology, new markets, new banking systems, new sources of raw materials, and increased wealth were all part of this revolution — the first of its kind in the world. The biggest change, however, was the huge increase in population, from 9 million in 1801 to 14 million in 1831 in England and Wales.

PUSHED OFF THE LAND

From the thirteenth century onward landlords in England had been enclosing common land to turn it into farmland. Cottagers and squatters who lived on the edge of open-field villages were driven out. The Enclosure Acts of the eighteenth century speeded up this process. Many of those who lost their homes and livelihoods crowded to areas where fields were still open or wandered as beggars. With the coming of the industrial revolution, many homeless country people joined the drift to the growing cities. By 1850 for the first time in Britain, more people lived in towns than in the country.

LIFE IN THE TOWNS

Factory owners built "back to back" terraced houses for their workers in the towns. These houses were damp, overcrowded, and had no drains or clean water supply. As many as three families might share a single room, especially in cities such as Manchester, Liverpool, and London, which attracted many poverty-stricken Irish immigrants. In the 1830s, 15 percent of the people of Liverpool lived in cellars, without light or heat. Diseases such as diphtheria, cholera, and tuberculosis were common.

> "In such places . . . I have seen the sick without beds, lying on rags. They can seldom afford straw."
>
> *Doctor's description of Manchester cellars, 1796*

Even in these miserable conditions, the threat of total homelessness was always present. If a man lost his job, he could be turned out of his home. Until the Poor Law Act was introduced by the government in 1834, homeless English workers could claim a small amount of help called outdoor relief, but after that date homeless people had to go to the workhouse. These institutions were dreaded by everybody. They were nicknamed "Bastille" because it was felt they were no better than the infamous French prison.

In the grim workhouse, families were separated, and husbands were kept apart from their wives and children. Mentally ill people, the sick, and the dying also often

This drawing of an inner city street in nineteenth century London shows that for many, the street was home. A doorway, cellar, or overcrowded room provided basic shelter rather than a home.

ended up in the workhouse too. There was little or no separate accommodation for these groups. Everyone who was not sick was put to work and given only the bare minimum of food. The shame and hopelessness of being in the workhouse was so great that many families chose to starve rather than enter its doors.

Some factory owners looked after their workers well, and built decent homes for them. But most people earned so little that it was impossible to keep some money in case of sickness or as security for old age. In addition, the very long working hours — often 15 or 16 hours a day — meant that most workers went home simply to sleep. Sometimes they even dropped with exhaustion where they were and slept in whatever quiet corner they could find. In conditions like these it was almost impossible to create anything in the way of a home or family life.

A STORY REPEATED

Today, "city drift," the flight of people from country to city, is just as marked in Third World countries as it was in eighteenth and nineteenth century Britain. As the populations of countries such as India, Brazil, and Kenya continue to grow, families can no longer make a living from the land. So they move to the city in search of a better life. There is no going back, as this story of Vijay shows.

Vijay had borrowed some money to start a cycle-repair business in his home village, but he was unable to keep up the repayments. He and his family had to sell their plot of land, which was too small to support them anyway. Vijay moved to Bombay in search of work, and stayed there, living on the streets with his wife and children. His pavement shelter was destroyed by the authorities in 1985, when the courts ruled that the landless squatters were illegally occupying valuable city land, and the local government of Bombay had the right to **evict** them.

TRAPPED ON THE SIDEWALKS

The homeless in Bombay and many other cities are used to their shacks being constantly demolished in so-called "cleaning-up" operations. They show great courage and endurance in constantly restarting their lives. Vijay, who rebuilt his hut, now works in the nearby industrial estate. He earns a small daily wage in a factory. His wife, Gita, works at home making incense holders, while looking after their four-month-old daughter. She earns an even smaller amount. Many street-dwellers recycle the waste products of society, such as waste paper or milk bottle tops. Many perform services that benefit the rich, which is why they live where they do, close to the city center. The problem is that they will never earn enough to afford alternative housing and find a way off the sidewalks.

CHILDREN OF THE STREETS

During the nineteenth century, a homeless child had various ways of surviving in the city. Begging in the streets was common, as well as some forms of crime. In *Oliver Twist*, the English Victorian writer Charles Dickens describes the lives of a group of child pickpockets, who work for their "minder" in return for food and shelter. Many homeless and orphaned children were rounded up and sent to work in factories. They had very few rights and many were cruelly treated and abused by their employers who literally owned them.

In the big cities of the industrialized world things slowly improved, and children began to be protected by new laws. However, today in other countries and newer cities, there are homeless children still struggling to survive in equally grim conditions. The children who sleep on the streets of Rio de Janeiro in Brazil have been numbered at more than 2,000. They have many different reasons for being there, but for all of them the streets of a big city provide their only hope of surviving, whether it is by begging, picking over garbage, stealing, or selling themselves as prostitutes.

A HELPING HAND?

There are individuals and organizations who try to help these children by providing food and shelter at day centers. But for the children themselves, the streets are home, and their family is their own group of street

The shanty town of El Mesquital in Guatemala. Families
began to settle here in 1984. Two years later, water was
provided — one tap for every 100 families. Thoughout the
world there are many such shanty towns with a shortage of
land to cultivate and even fewer job opportunities.

children. Many are killed in violent clean-up campaigns, because those who have jobs and homes simply see them as future criminals. One murdered street child was found on the beach in Rio with a sign saying "I killed you because you have no future."

Whatever help charities and volunteers can give these children, there is little real hope for them unless the root causes of their poverty and homelessness are tackled.

THE EARTH, OUR HOME

This photograph was taken in South Dakota in 1936. It shows an abandoned homestead and total destruction of a farming landscape from overuse.

Today, many people are beginning to look at the cost of development, or "progress" as it is sometimes called. The changes brought about by industrial revolutions in Europe and North America caused problems such as overcrowding in cities. It also made the world seem a smaller place. Trade opened up new markets in other countries. Many parts of the world were drawn into an unequal relationship with the industrialized countries.

The problems continue today. Producing wealth for some countries has meant cutting down forests in others. Changing production methods in order to create more food and other goods has led to the ruin of land and water in many parts of the world. Many people have been made homeless by these changes, too, as this chapter shows.

FATE OF THE GREAT PLAINS

The great Plains of North America stretch across Oklahoma, Texas, and parts of neighboring states. Before European settlers reached this area in the nineteenth century, the ground was covered with prairie grasses. This provided grazing for herds of wild buffalo.

Once the settler-farmers began to rear cattle on the land, the **ecology** of the plains changed. It changed still further when, in order to increase production, farmers began to plow up the land to sow winter wheat and other grain crops. The crops drained the goodness from the soil, and overgrazing by the cattle removed the grasses that held the soil together. Over a number of years this led to disaster, when in the mid 1930s, there was a terrible drought. The soil simply blew away in the strong winds, and the area became known as the Dust Bowl.

Many thousands of farmers were ruined. They were forced to abandon their homes and travel west in search of work. More than half the population left the area. Many homeless farmers and their families worked for starvation wages on California fruit farms or struggled to compete for work in the cities. Others ended up in charity relief camps. These were hard times for everybody in the United States, and there was not much sympathy for the victims of the drought.

A SHRINKING SEA

On the other side of the world, thousands of miles from midwest America, you will find the Aral Sea. It is one of the world's largest inland seas, and lies on the border of Kazakhstan and Uzbekistan, deep in the south of the former Soviet Union.

Fishermen used to live on the shores of the Aral. Now their boats are marooned on dry land. Half the sea has gone, drained for irrigation, and the rest is poisoned by pesticides. The fishermen used to catch 25,000 tons of fish a year until Soviet scientists decided to alter the flow of the rivers into the Aral in order to open up the area for intensive agriculture. Now, it seems the Aral Sea will never recover. Members of the fishing community must starve or move on. Their livelihood is gone.

SHRINKING FORESTS

In the basin of the Amazon River in Brazil, nearly 100 square miles of rainforest are cleared every year for cattle ranching. The timber from the trees is exported. The Amerindian peoples who live in the rainforest become more exposed to western diseases as their homes and their way of life are destroyed.

Often it is also the very poorest people themselves who are involved in clearing land from the rainforest. Many peasant farmers in Brazil and Guatemala, for example, have been forced off established farming areas by big landowners. The landowners want to use the land for growing crops such as coffee, tobacco, or pineapples that can be sold overseas. In order to carry on growing food for

"In my area we have about 15 products that we extract from the forest. . . . So I think this must be preserved. . . . When they think of felling trees, they always think of building roads, and the roads bring destruction under the mask of progress."

Jaime Araujo,
rubber tapper in the Amazon forest, 1987

This type of wasteland in the forests of Brazil was created by mining operations. The area is now uninhabitable for forest-dwelling Native Americans, and of little use for sustainable farming.

themselves and their families, the peasant farmers are forced to move into the forests and clear new land. The soil in these new areas is usually too poor to support years of cultivation, and so the farmers must move on again, leaving the dead land behind them. The only alternative is to join the already large numbers of homeless in the cities. So, in the forests of South America the needs of one group of homeless people directly threaten the homes of an even more vulnerable group.

Much of the best land is also taken for cash crops such as coffee and tea in Africa. As a result, people are crowded onto land that cannot support the population. Women are forced to walk farther and farther to fetch firewood and water, stripping the land of trees. Here, too, it is the poor who are pushed into farming the more difficult, or **marginal**, land in order to support themselves and their families in the traditional way.

CHANGING THE LANDSCAPE

Sometimes there are well-intentioned programs to increase food production and help people live more secure lives. But these, too, can go wrong. In the 1970s the Nigerian government decided to develop three huge irrigation plans in dry areas in the north of the country so that peasant farmers could grow a second crop of wheat as well as maize and sorghum. Building the dams meant flooding out thousands of people, who were promised they would get new houses and land.

In 1980 the Bakalori Dam on the Sokoto River was constructed, and the large trading center of Maradun was flooded. The dam engineers built the people a new town, New Maradun, but three years after the dam flooded their lands, the new houses stood empty because the people were not given land to go with their new homes. Instead many people were forced to sell their animals and try their luck in the cities of the south.

The farmers set up road blocks to try to stop the construction work on the dam, and the police and army were called in. Farmers were killed and several villages were burned. Even those who did receive new land found that they had more problems. The wheat they were supposed to be growing required heavy doses of expensive fertilizer. They could no longer grow sorghum to feed themselves, but had to buy it from the market. Farmers fell into debt when the wheat failed. For the first time people became landless and homeless in an area where they had always been able to feed themselves by traditional farming methods.

Downstream, the Kano River and Bakalori Dam prevented the rivers from flooding in the wet season, affecting a quarter of a million people. They were no longer able to grow tomatoes and peppers and make money from selling their crops. This came as a "surprise" to the experts.

Today many farmers are being ruined by the demands of this kind of **capitalist** farming development — agriculture for profit. When the poorer farmers cannot afford these methods they are pushed off the land. On top of this, the big international "agri-businesses" are using some of the best land in poorer countries to produce food for richer customers overseas. This is more profitable than the old system of growing and selling the basic food crops to local people, but it adds to their suffering.

DEAD LAND

The town of Chernobyl in the Ukraine is one of the most chilling reminders of how we can scar the earth and make it uninhabitable. Today Chernobyl is a ghost town. No one lives there. On April 26, 1986, one of the reactors in the nearby nuclear power station exploded, releasing a massive amount of radiation into the atmosphere. The town's 50,000 inhabitants were evacuated about 36 hours after the explosion. Since that date, many have fallen sick or have died in hospitals elsewhere from the result of their exposure to the radiation. Others have been rehoused; they are not homeless, but they cannot return to their home town because the environment has been poisoned and will remain a death trap for many years to come.

Parki, a settlement about 12 miles from Chernobyl. Within 36 hours of the nuclear explosion at Chernobyl in 1986, the 2,000 inhabitants of Parki had to leave their homes. This shows what remained four years later in 1990.

POWER AND POLITICS

This Aboriginal family are descendants of those who lost their way of life as a result of European settlement and "ownership" of land in Australia.

People often lose their homes for political reasons. This happens when governments make decisions based on religious and racial **prejudice**, or when they support the interests of one group against another.

THE THIRST FOR WEALTH

During the age of exploration in the fifteenth and sixteenth centuries, the governments of Europe encouraged and supported people to **colonize** the newly discovered lands. The wealth of the colonies, such as minerals, timber and crops, were all used to make the colonizing countries richer and more powerful. The lives of the **indigenous** peoples in Africa, Asia, and the Americas were greatly changed by this process.

CLASH OF CULTURES

Aboriginal peoples have lived in Australia since the Stone Age more than 10,000 years ago. They wandered freely across a network of "lines" across the plains and deserts of Australia. These special routes were often marked by sacred places along the way. The Aboriginals called them "footprints of the ancestors," or "dreaming tracks."

To the Europeans who settled in Australia from the eighteenth century onward the land was rich and ready for development. Huge areas were fenced off for farming, European style. Mines were dug, minerals extracted. As the European population grew, the Aboriginals were robbed of their own space and their freedom to wander.

In the late 1950s the Pintupi were the last Aboriginal tribe to be brought out of the Western Desert. Previously they had lived off the land. The men hunted emu and kangaroo and the women gathered seeds, roots, and edible grubs. When the government rounded them up they were sent to Popanji, west of Alice Springs, where many suffered and even died because of dirt, disease and violence.

In losing their land and its sacred sites, the Aboriginals lost much of their way of life. The Australian government gave them settlements to live in, which were exactly the opposite of the Aboriginal idea of home.

It is 1983 and the South African police are supervising the destruction of an illegal settlement outside Capetown. The women in the foreground have made themselves a temporary barricade out of their belongings, but they will be moved on within a few hours.

EXILED TO HOMELANDS

South Africa has also had a long history of conflict over land. European settlers and their descendants struggled with each other over land. They fought wars and crushed African resistance to their increasing control over the country.

Throughout the twentieth century, Africans in South Africa have had their rights to homes and land removed by the white European-only government. Laws of **apartheid**, or separate development, ensured that Africans were kept apart from whites in every aspect of their daily lives except in the course of their employment as workers.

In 1959, the system of apartheid was strengthened even more. Bantustans, or "homelands," were created for the African population. The first homeland to be established was Transkei. Another was Bophuthatswana, made up of many unconnected pieces of land.

Although the Bantustans were called "homelands," in fact they were the opposite. Many Africans were evicted from their existing homes and herded into the new areas, often hundreds of miles away. Here, the soil, which was often poor, became worse through overcrowding. It was often impossible to farm. Although Africans who had work in the cities could remain outside the homelands, they were forbidden to live in city centers or white suburbs. Instead, they were confined to the African townships like Soweto outside Johannesburg. Unofficial African **shanty towns** outside cities such as Capetown were constantly under threat from police raids. Individuals who had no proof of employment had to leave for the homelands. Sometimes whole neighborhoods had their shelters bulldozed to the ground.

After more than 40 years in power, the nationalist government in South Africa is finally bowing to pressure from inside and outside the country. Apartheid and its laws have been withdrawn. However, for the thousands of Africans divided and trapped in poverty in the townships and the homelands, it is not yet clear what the future holds.

PALESTINE: WHOSE HOME?

"His Majesty's Government view with favour the establishment in Palestine of a national home for the Jewish people, and will use their best endeavours to facilitate the achievement of this object, it being clearly understood that nothing shall be done which may prejudice the civil and religious rights of existing non-Jewish communities in Palestine ..."

A.J. Balfour, British Foreign Secretary, 1917

In the 30 years that followed this statement, Jewish immigration to Palestine was hugely increased by the events of World War II in Europe. Thousands of Jews fled from persecution by the Nazis in Germany and the countries of eastern Europe. They turned to their "national home" in Palestine, the country around their holy city of Jerusalem.

Palestine was not an empty land. It was inhabited by over 5 million Palestinian Arabs who had lived there for generations. By 1947 the United Nations agreed that the pressures were so great that Palestine should be divided into two states, one Arab, one Jewish. And so the state of Israel was born, while the remaining part of Palestine became part of neighboring Jordan.

During the following year, 1948, the Israelis put into practice their plan to evict the Arabs from Palestine. The terror of this campaign caused nearly one million Palestinians to flee from the homes they had occupied for generations. Some of them were able to settle in Jordan and other Arab countries such as Lebanon and Syria. Others still live in refugee camps, more than 40 years after being made homeless. Israel has so far refused to allow them to return or to receive **compensation** for their lost homes and land, in spite of repeated demands for this from the United Nations.

Since 1967, when Israeli troops occupied the West Bank of the Jordan River and the Gaza Strip, more Palestinian villages have been destroyed to make way for new Israeli settlements. In 1987 the Palestinians began the *intifadah*, or uprising, in protest. Since that date increasing numbers of Palestinian houses have been demolished or sealed by the military authorities in the occupied territories. In Palestinian villages such as Silwan, outside Jerusalem, extremist religious groups have confiscated and moved into Arab homes.

NEW COUNTRIES, NEW BARRIERS
Britain was a leading world power at the beginning of the twentieth century. It used its influence in an attempt to create a home for the Jews of Europe in Palestine. The resulting problems show how decisions of this sort can cause suffering for generations to come.

However, political power does not always stay in the same hands. People find themselves pushed together under new governments, then after a few generations, things change again. This has happened in the former Soviet Union, and in a number of eastern European countries that used to be under its influence. **Communism**, the political theory that held this huge part of the world together for over 80 years, has collapsed. It has been widely replaced by strong nationalistic ideas. Old hatreds have once more come to the surface, as people have tried to redraw their boundaries where they were many years ago. In Yugoslavia, this has led to the forced removal of thousands of people from areas where it is felt they don't "belong." They, too, find themselves homeless in what was once their own country.

NO EASY ANSWERS

As the chapters in this book have shown, there are many forces that drive people from their homes. Sometimes the homelessness is temporary, and people are able to rebuild their homes and lives and start again. Sometimes, though, there is no quick solution, and people spend many years, even their whole lives, in conditions of homelessness.

It is a problem that knows no boundaries of nation or race. One-tenth of the world's population lives illegally in inner-city squats or shanty towns. Worldwide there are 20 million refugees who have fled their homes. In the rich cities of the world such as London and New York, increasing numbers of homeless people sleep in doorways or shelter in empty buildings that they cannot afford to rent or buy.

Homelessness is now a problem in the former communist countries, too, where it has shown up earlier evils. In Russia, many of the homeless children on the streets of St. Petersburg were once housed in state-run orphanages. Now they have run away from the terror of these institutions, where they were often falsely classified as mentally backward so they could be locked away from the rest of the world.

In all these situations there are individuals and

A tank remains in the background while a woman gathers up her precious possessions in Bosnia, part of the former country of Yugoslavia. Like many others, she is caught up in the violence between the many different national and ethnic groups that once made up the country.

organizations who do their best to ease the suffering and provide some comfort, but there are no easy answers. Homelessness is part of a much larger problem. The gap between the living standards of the rich and poor countries of the world continues to widen, and within the rich countries the situation of the very poorest and weakest groups is becoming steadily worse.

> "All things are connected like the blood which unites one family . . . man did not weave the web of life: he is merely a strand in it. Whatever he does to the web, he does to himself."
>
> *From Chief Seattle's reply to a U.S. government offer for Indian land, 1854*

Shelter is a basic human right. Unless governments pay more attention to this in their own countries, there will be an increase in the violence and crime that so often results from feelings of desperation and hopelessness. On an international level, we all need to cooperate in preserving the environment. Development and growth has to be on a scale that we can support, together, not simply to provide quick riches for a few countries. It is a big challenge, but it is possible.

KEY DATES

448 B.C.
Driving out the defeated: Athenian forces expel islanders of Evvoia and replace them with their own people.

A.D. 79
Homes buried: Mount Vesuvius destroys the town of Pompeii.

1344–1348
Plague: Survivors forced to leave homes throughout Europe after destruction of village communities by plague.

1631
Destroyed by siege: City of Magdeburg burned and survivors made homeless by one of many events in the Thirty Years' War.

1666
Fire! Great fire of London destroys many homes, but buildings are replaced and improved.

1700s
Speeding up evictions: Land enclosures by Acts of Parliament enable large landowners to overrule or evict smaller ones more easily.

1834
Forced into the workhouse: The Poor Law Act removes all relief for the homeless in Britain and Ireland.

1846
No food, no home: The potato famine in Ireland forces thousands to move out in search of food.

1906
A city collapses: Many homes destroyed in San Francisco earthquake.

1935
The Dust Bowl: Farmland destroyed in Oklahoma. Farmers ruined, forced to move out.

1940
Homeless underground: Civilians shelter from successive nights of enemy bombing in the "Blitz," which destroys many homes.

1945
Cry for Hiroshima: Entire city wiped out by first use of atomic bomb. Thousands killed or homeless.

1948
To share or not to share? Israel starts campaign to drive out Palestinians from shared territory.

1958–1959
Resettlement disaster: Last of the Aboriginal peoples — the Pintupi — removed from the desert to impoverished western settlement.

1986
Dead land: Accident at Chernobyl nuclear power plant wipes out whole area for foreseeable future habitation.

1992
Action? First world conference on the environment in Rio de Janeiro, a city with one of the highest homeless populations.

GLOSSARY

apartheid: Keeping races of a country separate from each other by force or law.

capitalism: An economic system in which land, factories, and firms are privately owned, and the owners of "capital," or wealth, control the production of goods for profit.

civil war: War between people of the same country.

colonize: Establish a settlement in a new country.

communism: A political theory based on the idea of common ownership of wealth. In the world's main communist countries (China and the former Soviet Union) wealth and property were taken over by the state and political power was kept firmly in the hands of the communist parties themselves.

compensation: Money paid out to people to make up for a loss or injury they have suffered.

ecology: Relationship between different living things and their surroundings.

environment: Surroundings and circumstances in which a person lives.

evacuate: To take people from a place where there is danger. Mass evacuations are usually organized by governments, who are responsible for arranging transportation, food, and accommodation for the people.

evict: To remove people from land or property by legal or illegal force.

extended family: Family grouping that includes many relations such as cousins, aunts, or uncles and covers more than two generations.

First World: The rich countries of the world such as France, Britain, and the United States. Also referred to as "the North," since most of these countries are in the northern half of the globe.

indigenous: Having lived in an area, country, or continent for many generations.

industrial revolution: A period in European history from about 1760 to about 1880 when industry was introduced and developed on a large scale. Industrialization happened more quickly in Britain than elsewhere in Europe, but many countries had big increases in population at this time.

marginal (of land): Only just able to support settled farming.

Middle Ages: A period in European history between "ancient" and "modern" times, usually considered to be from about 1000–1500.

nomad: People who move from place to place to find water and crops for their animals.

nuclear family: Family grouping consisting of parents and their children only. Most commonly found in the richer countries of the world.

plague: A disease carried by rats that can kill the victim within a few days without treatment. Outbreaks in the sixth and fourteenth centuries killed millions. Today the disease can be treated, and outbreaks have been smaller.

prejudice: Opinions based on false beliefs, which are often passed on from one person to another.

radiation: Harmful effect of rays released by a nuclear or atomic explosion.

segregate: Keeping people separate, usually along lines of race, sex, or religion.

shanty town: Makeshift town with shelters made from whatever waste materials are available such as old timber, bits of cardboard, plastic sheeting, or iron scraps.

squatter: Someone who occupies a property or a piece of land illegally. In many cities people "squat" in empty buildings or build their own camps on the edge of town.

Third World: Poor countries of the world such as India, Bangladesh, and Ethiopia. Also known as "the South" since most of them are in the southern half of the globe.

INDEX